CON...

Tick the circles when you have spotted the species.

ALL ABOUT INSECTS

Insects are by far the most common type of animal. More than nine out of ten living species are insects. They flourish in nearly every part of the world, except under the sea and in the very coldest places. Insects are so successful because of their powerful exoskeletons (outer casing), ability to fly and small size.

Butterflies & moths have scaly wings. There may be 200 to 600 scales on every square millimetre of wing.

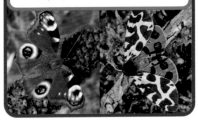

Ants, bees & wasps belong to the same insect group, and ants are one of the most successful insects on Earth.

Bugs have piercing and sucking mouthparts. They can be just a few millimetres long or giant water bugs.

Flies have large compound eyes made up of many indivdual lenses. True flies only have one pair of wings.

Beetles are the most successful animal group on Earth. There are at least 360,000 species of beetle.

Other insects include lacewings and dragonflies. There are between one and eight million species of insect.

ANATOMY

Insects have bodies that are dived into three segments: the head, the thorax and the abdomen. Three pairs of legs are attached to the thorax, and, if there are any, wings too. The heads have the sensory organs, such as eyes and antennae.

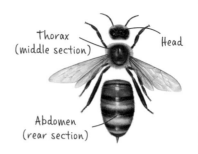

Thorax (middle section)

Head

Abdomen (rear section)

The mouthparts are adapted to different feeding methods, such as chewing, biting, stabbing and sucking

Two antennae on the insect's head are used to sense smell, touch and sound

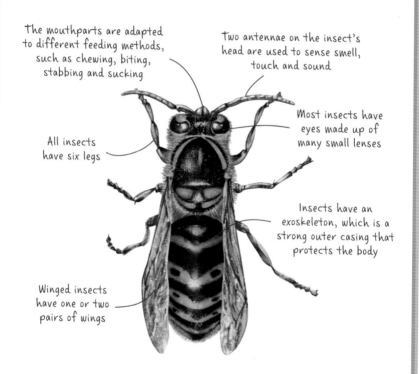

Most insects have eyes made up of many small lenses

All insects have six legs

Insects have an exoskeleton, which is a strong outer casing that protects the body

Winged insects have one or two pairs of wings

Male ♂

♀ Female

Where possible, symbols have been used to show if an insect is male or female. The symbol ♂ means male and ♀ means female.

BRIMSTONE

Brimstone butterflies are widespread around Britain and other parts of Europe and North Africa. The bluish-green larvae (caterpillars) feed on buckthorn and alder buckthorn leaves. The adults live on a diet of nectar, which they suck from flowers such as buddleia. Adults emerge from their chrysalises in July and live until the following summer, following a winter hibernation. The females lay their eggs on the underside of buckthorn leaves.

ACTUAL SIZE

Butterflies may have been named after these yellow insects. Or perhaps from an ancient myth, which held that witches changed into butterflies to steal butter.

FACT FILE

Scientific name
Gonepteryx rhamni

Habitat Woodland and scrub

Breeding Eggs are laid in May, larvae pupate in June/July and adults emerge two weeks later

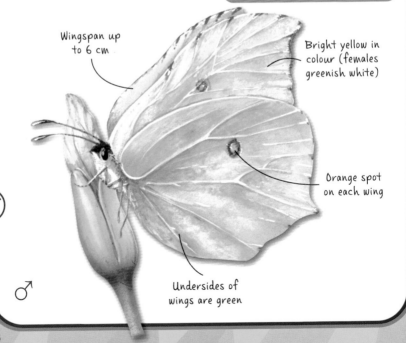

Wingspan up to 6 cm

Bright yellow in colour (females greenish white)

Orange spot on each wing

♂

Undersides of wings are green

CABBAGE WHITE

These are small white, cream or pale yellow butterflies. Females have two black spots on each of their forewings and males have just one. They live in gardens, meadows and fields. Adults suck nectar from flowers, such as dandelions, and the larvae eat leaves of plants from the mustard family, such as cabbage, broccoli and cauliflower. Adults can often be seen in mating rituals, flying upwards in spirals.

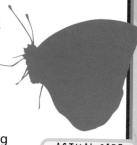

ACTUAL SIZE

Adult butterflies emerge from their pupae in July. They breed twice in summer and the last generation spends winter, protected from cold, as a pupa or chrysalis.

FACT FILE

Scientific name *Pieris rapae*

Habitat Gardens and fields

Breeding The larvae are green with black stripes on their backs and sides

Two black spots on each forewing

Soft body covered with bristles

4.5 cm wingspan

♀

7

COMMA

With dull patterns on the underside of their wings, commas can be difficult to see among dead leaves. This camouflage helps to protect the butterflies from predators, such as birds and bats, when they overwinter and hang from leaves. Commas live in gardens, hedges and woodlands. There they can find flowers that supply them with nectar as adults, and leaves such as stinging nettles, which provide food for larvae.

ACTUAL SIZE

The larvae are black with red-and-white markings, giving them the appearance of bird droppings. They are covered in spines.

FACT FILE

Scientific name
Polygonia c-album

Habitat Gardens and meadows

Breeding Two broods each year

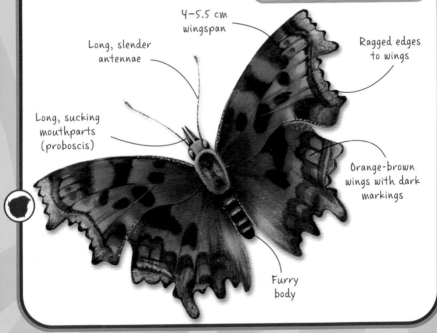

4–5.5 cm wingspan

Long, slender antennae

Long, sucking mouthparts (proboscis)

Ragged edges to wings

Orange-brown wings with dark markings

Furry body

COMMON BLUE

Th{
These pretty butterflies are most likely to be seen between May and September, when they feed on nectar.} They are most common around large, flat-headed flowers, especially near roadsides or meadows. The larvae are green with yellow stripes along their sides and a dark line down their backs. They feed on the leaves of plants, such as white clover and bird's-foot trefoil.

ACTUAL SIZE

The larvae produce a substance from their skin that attracts ants, and in turn, the ants protect the larvae from predators.

FACT FILE

Scientific name
Polyommatus icarus

Habitat Grasslands, dunes and wastelands

Breeding Larvae are small and green

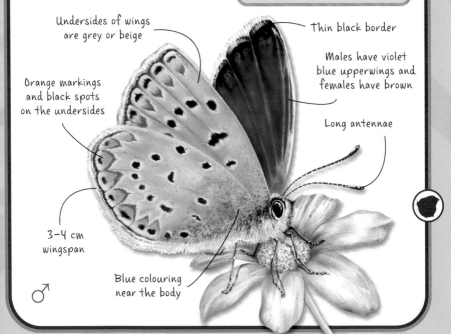

Undersides of wings are grey or beige

Thin black border

Males have violet blue upperwings and females have brown

Orange markings and black spots on the undersides

Long antennae

3–4 cm wingspan

♂

Blue colouring near the body

HOLLY BLUE

Holly blue butterflies are found flying around holly bushes in spring, where the females lay their eggs. The larvae, which are small and green, feed on holly flower buds. When they mature, this first brood mates to produce a second brood. This time, the eggs are usually laid on ivy. This second group of adults is able to survive winter as chrysalises, or pupae.

ACTUAL SIZE

Adult holly blues feed on sap from plants and the sticky substance made by aphids.

FACT FILE

Scientific name
Celastrina argiolus

Habitat Woodlands, parks and gardens

Breeding Two broods every summer

3–4 cm wingspan

Antennae have small white stripes

Underside of wings is pale grey/blue with black spots

Broad black borders to wings in females (narrower in males)

Pale, violet blue wings

♀

ORANGE TIP

These colourful butterflies flit around flowers in early summer, from April to June, laying their eggs. The pale eggs are long and thin, but turn orange after a few days. The green larvae feed on the flowerbuds, but they will eat each other if they can. The orange tips on the males' forewings warn birds that they taste bad.

ACTUAL SIZE

Only one egg is laid at a time, so it can take a female some time to lay her whole clutch on the undersides of flowerbuds.

FACT FILE

Scientific name
Anthocharis cardamines

Habitat Gardens, meadows and hedgerows

Breeding Lays single eggs

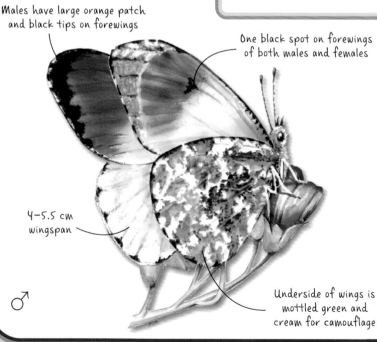

Males have large orange patch and black tips on forewings

One black spot on forewings of both males and females

4–5.5 cm wingspan

♂

Underside of wings is mottled green and cream for camouflage

PEACOCK

Peacock butterflies are often seen on buddleia in summer. They wake from hibernation in spring and soon mate. Females lay small green eggs in batches of up to 500, often on nettles or hops, the larvae's favourite food. Adults emerge from the pupae in July and feed on nectar from flowers, or suck the juice from over-ripe fruit. The life expectancy of adults is one year.

ACTUAL SIZE

Peacock butterflies get their name from the large, eye-like patterns on their wings, which are similar to the eye-shaped patterns on the tails of peacock birds.

FACT FILE

Scientific name *Inachis io*

Habitat Flowery gardens and meadows

Breeding Fully grown larvae are about 4 cm long and they have black-and-white spots and long, black dorsal spines

Hair on thorax

Long antennae used for smelling and touching

5–7.5 cm wingspan

Four false eyes on wings

Dark brown wing edges

RED ADMIRAL

Named after their 'admirable' colours, these butterflies are easily recognized by their dark-coloured wings with red bands and white spots. They have hints of blue and black spots on their hindwings. Red admirals are fast, powerful flyers and – unusually for butterflies – may fly at night. These insects are found throughout the UK and Europe and inhabit gardens, parks, woodlands, seashores and mountains.

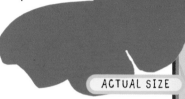

ACTUAL SIZE

The larvae of red admirals are normally dark and bristled, but the colour varies from green–grey–black with yellow lines on either side.

FACT FILE

Scientific name
Vanessa atalanta

Habitat Gardens and meadows

Breeding Eggs are laid singularly on nettle leaves

Red bands on forewings

Long antennae

6 cm wingspan

Red patches along the back of hindwings

Edges of wings lined with blue spots

SMALL TORTOISESHELL

Named after their colouring, small tortoiseshells are often one of the first types of butterfly to be seen in spring. Adults emerge from hibernation in March or April and mate soon afterwards. They lay their eggs on food plants, such as nettles, and they hatch about ten days later. Small tortoiseshells are common butterflies and live in a range of habitats, particularly near human homes.

ACTUAL SIZE

This butterfly's Latin name, *Aglais urticae*, comes from the word for nettles, *urtica*, the butterfly's favourite food.

FACT FILE

Scientific name *Aglais urticae*

Habitat Flowery gardens and meadows

Breeding Heaps of eggs are laid on the underside of nettle leaves in April

Blue markings along wing edges

4–5.5 cm wingspan

Points on the edges of forewings and hindwings

Orange-and-black markings on wings

SPECKLED WOOD

Speckled wood butterflies fly around woodlands and gardens in the summer months. They do not surround flowers (like many other butterflies do) because they do not feed on nectar, but on the sugary substance that aphids make. Females lay single eggs on grasses, which the larvae feed on when they hatch. The larvae eat and moult for about ten days before turning into chrysalises.

ACTUAL SIZE

Males fiercely defend their territories from rival males. They can sometimes be seen fighting, with their wings clashing.

FACT FILE

Scientific name
Pararge aegeria

Habitat Woodlands and gardens

Breeding Larvae are green

4 cm wingspan

Wings are mottled brown with creamy markings

Slender antennae

Brown furry body

Undersides are orange, brown and yellow

Forewings have one black eyespot

Hindwings have a row of three black eyespots

SWALLOWTAIL

Swallowtails are Britain's largest butterflies and amongst the most attractive. Their name describes the long 'tails' that grow at the back of the hindwings. The larvae are black and white and resemble bird droppings, which protects them from predators. As they grow they turn green and black, with orange marks, and produce a foul smell to keep predators at bay. The adults feed on nectar and the larvae feed only on milk parsley.

ACTUAL SIZE

Swallowtails were once common in many British marshlands, but are now found only in the marshes around the Norfolk Broads.

FACT FILE

Scientific name
Papilio machaon

Habitat Marshland

Breeding Eggs are laid in several broods from April–September and they may hatch the same year, or the next

Yellow wings with black veins

Wingspan up to 8 cm

Long, black tails

Hindwings have a band of blue and a red spot

CODLING MOTH

The larvae of the codling moth are pests that eat the fruit of some trees, particularly apple and pear. Adult females lay a single egg on a leaf of the tree. When the larva emerges, it bores into apples or pears, making long tunnels as it eats its way through the fruit flesh. The larva pupates under bark or in leaf litter, emerging as an adult between November and February, depending on the conditions.

ACTUAL SIZE

The large eye-shaped markings on the tips of the codling moth's forewings distract and confuse predators, such as birds.

FACT FILE

Scientific name
Cydia pomonella

Habitat Where apple trees grow

Breeding Larvae are also known as apple maggots and they have white bodies and brown heads

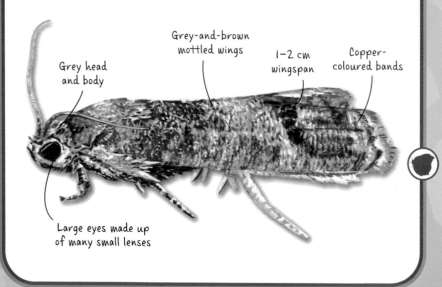

Grey-and-brown mottled wings

1-2 cm wingspan

Copper-coloured bands

Grey head and body

Large eyes made up of many small lenses

DEATH'S HEAD HAWK MOTH

This striking species of moth gets its name from the unusual pattern on the back of its thorax. This is the part of the body between the head and the fleshy abdomen. The pattern resembles a skull, which is also known as a 'death's head'. These moths are not native to Britain, but migrate here for the summer. The larvae feed on potato plants, so the adults are more likely to be found in farms than in woods or gardens.

SCALE

FACT FILE

Scientific name
Acherontia atropos

Habitat Farmland

Breeding The pale green larvae have purple and white stripes, and can grow up to 15 cm in length

These moths have the strange habit of crawling into beehives in search of honey. They can produce a loud squeaking noise if they are handled or startled.

Wingspan up to 14 cm

Large eyes

Thorax with skull-like pattern

Thick body

Wings have dark mottled pattern in cream, tans and browns

GARDEN TIGER MOTH

Garden tiger moths are very common and easy to spot with their bold colours. The red-coloured hindwings warn other animals that they taste bad and to leave them alone. Garden tigers feed on nectar from flowers. The larvae are brown and black, and are so hairy they have been given the name of 'woolly bears'. The hairs cause irritation, so they protect the larvae from hungry birds.

ACTUAL SIZE

Garden tiger moths are very variable in appearance and it is rare to find two moths with exactly the same markings.

FACT FILE

Scientific name *Arctia caja*

Habitat Gardens, farms and open areas

Breeding Black and orange larvae

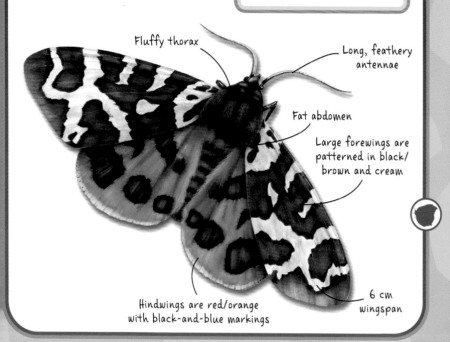

Fluffy thorax

Long, feathery antennae

Fat abdomen

Large forewings are patterned in black/ brown and cream

Hindwings are red/orange with black-and-blue markings

6 cm wingspan

MAGPIE MOTH

Boldly patterned, magpie moths have **black-and-white wings with yellow bands.** This colouring warns predators, such as birds and spiders, that they taste foul. The adults emerge from their pupae in June and drink nectar from flowers. They can be seen until August and, unlike many other moths, they are active during the day.

ACTUAL SIZE

Moths and butterflies belong to the same insect family. However moths usually have drab colours, are active at night and have thick or feathery antennae.

FACT FILE

Scientific name
Abraxas grossulariata

Habitat Meadows and woods

Breeding Larvae feed on various shrubs

Forewings are white with black bands and spots

Long antennae

4–5 cm wingspan

Orange band crosses the forewings

APHID

There are about 4000 types of aphid and many of those are garden pests. The most well-known aphid is the common greenfly, which lives on plants. Aphids use their long, slender mouthparts to pierce a hole in the stems of plants. Then they eat the liquid food that pours out of the hole. Aphids also damage plants by passing viruses between them. Ladybirds and lacewings are predators of aphids.

ACTUAL SIZE

Aphids produce a sticky substance called honeydew, which ants collect for food. In return, the ants protect the aphids from other predators.

FACT FILE

Scientific name
Aphidae family

Habitat Tender plant stems, leaves and buds

Breeding Seasonal

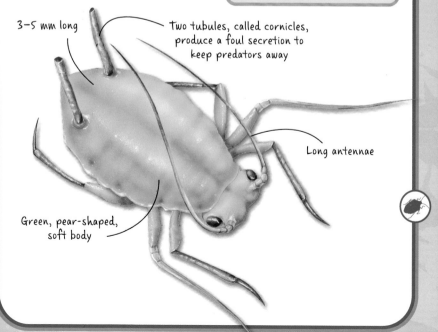

3–5 mm long

Two tubules, called cornicles, produce a foul secretion to keep predators away

Long antennae

Green, pear-shaped, soft body

COMMON GREEN CAPSID

It may not be easy to see capsids, but the damage they do to fruit crops is often obvious. When they feed on fruits, such as apples, pears and strawberries, capsids leave small brown spots, which lead to strange-looking fruits. The nymphs look like their parents and they feed on the new shoots growing on the plants.

ACTUAL SIZE

FACT FILE

Scientific name
Lygocoris pabulinus

Habitat Anywhere there are plants

Breeding Lays eggs on plants

Female capsids lay their eggs on fruit tree leaves in spring and they hatch after just two weeks.

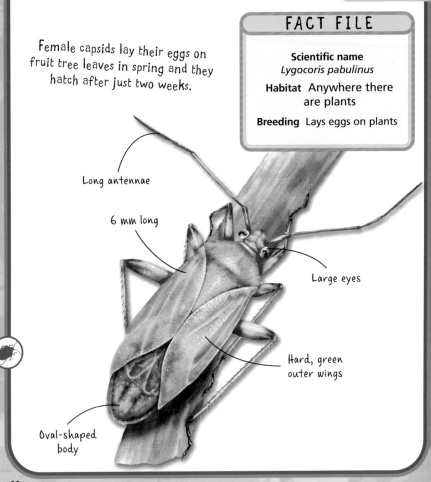

Long antennae

6 mm long

Large eyes

Hard, green
outer wings

Oval-shaped
body

FIREBUG

Firebugs are easy to spot because of the interesting red-and-black pattern on their backs. They mostly eat seeds, but they can also attack and eat small insects. Firebugs are most likely to be found on lime or marrow trees, as they particularly like their seeds. The adults hibernate over winter, so they are ready to mate in spring or early summer. The eggs hatch to produce nymphs that look like the adults.

ACTUAL SIZE

Most firebugs do not fly, but occasionally some develop long hindwings that can be used for flight.

FACT FILE

Scientific name
Pyrrhocoris apterus

Habitat Grasslands and any open land

Breeding Mate in spring or early summer

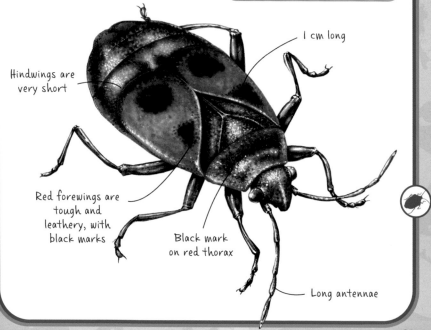

I cm long

Hindwings are very short

Red forewings are tough and leathery, with black marks

Black mark on red thorax

Long antennae

GREEN SHIELD BUG

Often found resting on leaves in the sun, green shield bugs are broad and flat in shape. They have hard forewings that protect the second pair of wings. Their sucking mouthparts are used to drink sap from plants. The larvae are similar in shape to adults, but they are black and green. Adults spend winter hibernating in leaf litter and in spring, females lay up to 400 eggs on plants.

ACTUAL SIZE

Shield bugs may look like beetles, but actually they belong to a different group of insects called bugs, or hemipterans.

FACT FILE

Scientific name
Palomena prasina

Habitat Shrubs in gardens, woods and parks

Breeding Larvae are called nymphs

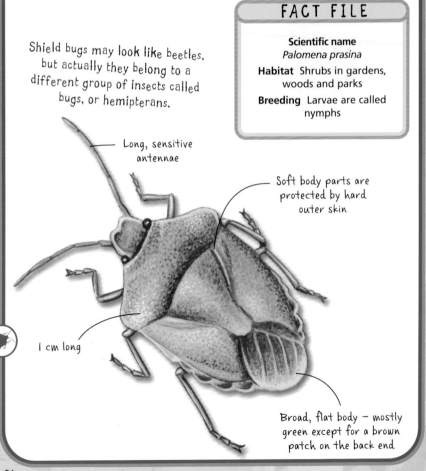

Long, sensitive antennae

Soft body parts are protected by hard outer skin

I cm long

Broad, flat body — mostly green except for a brown patch on the back end

LESSER WATER BOATMAN

These bugs swim in ponds and eat plant matter, often scraping algae off rocks or other surfaces. They use their unusually long legs like paddles as they move swiftly through the water. They are preyed upon by animals, such as dragonfly larvae and birds. Although lesser water boatmen look similar to water boatmen, or common backswimmers, they actually belong to a different group of bugs.

ACTUAL SIZE

Lesser water boatmen swim on their fronts, while water boatmen swim on their backs and are predators, hunting tadpoles, small fish and flying insects that fall in the water.

FACT FILE

Scientific name
Corixa punctata
Habitat Ponds and canals
Breeding Eggs are laid in spring and are attached to plants

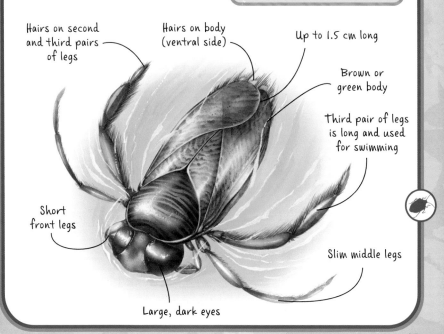

Hairs on second and third pairs of legs

Hairs on body (ventral side)

Up to 1.5 cm long

Brown or green body

Third pair of legs is long and used for swimming

Short front legs

Slim middle legs

Large, dark eyes

POND SKATER

Pond skaters are fascinating creatures to watch as they speed across the surface of the water without breaking its surface. These bugs are also known as waterstriders and they are widespread throughout Britain.

Pond skaters can detect prey by sensing vibrations on the water surface caused when an insect falls into the water. Within seconds, the pond skater has located its prey and grabs it with its short, stout front legs. If attacked themselves, they can jump out of danger.

ACTUAL SIZE

Pond skaters avoid freezing to death on ice-covered water by hibernating in the winter. They fly long distances to find a safe resting place until April.

FACT FILE

Scientific name *Gerris lacustris*

Habitat Ponds and still waters

Breeding Males and females mate on the surface of the water and the female lays her eggs on land

2 cm long, narrow body

Brown or dark grey body

Round eyes

Second and third pairs of legs are long and widely spaced (to balance bug on water)

Velvety, water-repelling hairs cover body and legs

WATER SCORPION

Water scorpions have wings, but they rarely fly. They live under the surface of shallow water and may be seen clinging to plants at the water's edge. Water scorpions breathe air and use long spikes from their abdomens like snorkels, taking air from above the water's surface. They can also hold bubbles of air in hairs below their wings.

ACTUAL SIZE

Water scorpions use their strong front limbs to grab prey, such as tadpoles and small fish.

FACT FILE

Scientific name
Nepa cinerea

Habitat Ponds

Breeding Eggs laid in pond plants

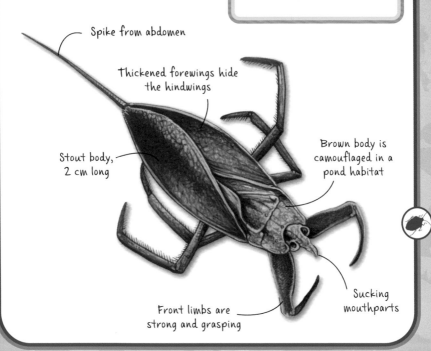

Spike from abdomen

Thickened forewings hide the hindwings

Stout body, 2 cm long

Brown body is camouflaged in a pond habitat

Front limbs are strong and grasping

Sucking mouthparts

BLOODY-NOSED BEETLE

Bloody-nosed beetles are widespread in **Britain, especially southern areas.** However they are hard to spot because, like many other beetles, they are secretive animals. They can be found in hedgerows or other sheltered areas, and they are most active at night, although they can be seen scuttling around on hot summer days. These large beetles feed on the leaves of low-growing plants and hibernate until April, to avoid the cold winter months when food is in short supply.

ACTUAL SIZE

These beetles get their name from their unusual form of defence. If attacked, they produce a red fluid from their mouth, which scares the predator and tastes bitter.

FACT FILE

Scientific name
Timarcha tenebricosa

Habitat Woodlands, farms, parks and heaths

Breeding Bluish-black larvae hatch in April, spend the summer eating, then mature into adults

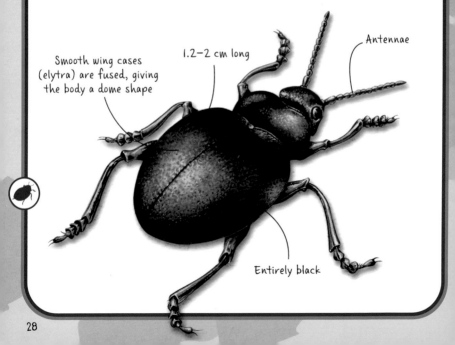

Smooth wing cases (elytra) are fused, giving the body a dome shape

1.2–2 cm long

Antennae

Entirely black

BOMBARDIER BEETLE

Like all ground beetles, bombardier beetles lay their eggs where the newly hatched grubs will find food, such as in a pile of rotting leaves. The grubs grow quickly and moult, or shed, their skin as they get bigger. Eventually they pupate, and during this time of change, the grub grows into an adult beetle. Bombardier beetles cannot fly. To defend themselves from predators, they spray a burning liquid from their rear ends.

ACTUAL SIZE

The chemicals needed to produce this beetle's burning fluid are stored in the abdomen. They mix together in a special chamber just before being sprayed at a predator.

FACT FILE

Scientific name
Caribidae family

Habitat Woodlands and gardens

Breeding Larvae are called grubs

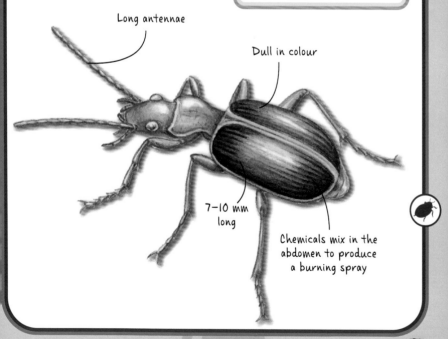

Long antennae

Dull in colour

7–10 mm long

Chemicals mix in the abdomen to produce a burning spray

CARDINAL BEETLE

These beetles are very distinctive and easy to identify. Their bodies are long, flattened and bright red, and their heads are either black or red. The hard outer casing on their bodies is formed of the forewings, which cover and protect the soft abdomen and second pair of wings underneath. Cardinal beetles fly from May to July and can sometimes be spotted on flowers or resting on tree trunks, particularly at the edges of woodlands.

ACTUAL SIZE

Black-headed cardinal beetles are most common in Wales and the Midlands, but the red-headed cardinal beetle is common throughout Britain.

FACT FILE

Scientific name
Pyrochroa coccinea
Habitat Woodland
Breeding Larvae are yellowish-brown and live under bark

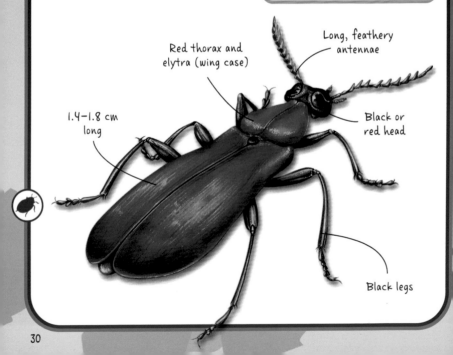

Red thorax and elytra (wing case)

Long, feathery antennae

1.4–1.8 cm long

Black or red head

Black legs

LADYBIRD

Brightly coloured beetles, ladybirds have round bodies and hard wing cases, called elytra. Adults spend winter in large groups, hidden under loose bark on trees or crammed into crevices. Ladybird larvae hatch from small eggs that are glued to plants either singly or in small groups. They mostly eat other soft-bodied animals. Thirteen-spot and five-spot ladybirds are very rare and seldom seen in the UK. The two-spot ladybird is smaller than its seven-spotted cousin.

ACTUAL SIZE

When handled, ladybirds produce drops of smelly yellow fluid from their legs to deter predators. Their bright colours also warn predators to stay away.

FACT FILE

Scientific name
Coccinella 7-punctata

Habitat Gardens and woodlands

Breeding Blue larvae with cream spots

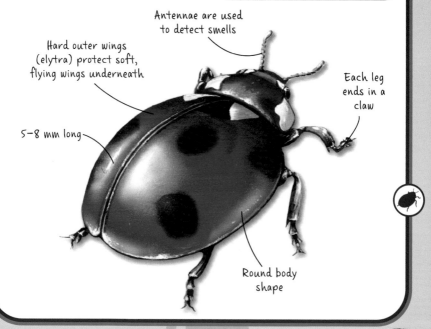

Antennae are used to detect smells

Hard outer wings (elytra) protect soft, flying wings underneath

Each leg ends in a claw

5–8 mm long

Round body shape

STAG BEETLE

One of the largest and most impressive insects, stag beetles can be heard as they noisily fly at dusk, searching for mates. Adults may only live for a few months and can survive without feeding. Males have large mouthparts called mandibles, which they use to fight one another for females. Gardens with undisturbed areas of rotting wood may attract these endangered animals, as the larvae feed on wood.

ACTUAL SIZE

Stag beetles were common in gardens and parklands, but they have become increasingly rare over the last 50 years and are now threatened with extinction.

FACT FILE

Scientific name
Lucanus cervus

Habitat Woodlands and gardens

Breeding White larvae with brown heads

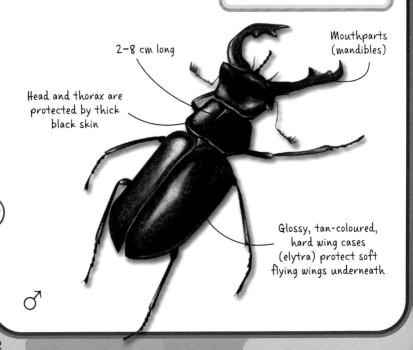

2–8 cm long

Mouthparts (mandibles)

Head and thorax are protected by thick black skin

Glossy, tan-coloured, hard wing cases (elytra) protect soft flying wings underneath

♂

ANT

Found in almost every habitat on land in the world, ants live in large colonies. They can be seen busily scurrying around a garden from spring to autumn, but are seen less often in winter when the temperatures are low. A colony of ants is divided into different types – the queen ant, female workers and male ants. Some defend the nest, for example, while others are involved in reproduction.

ACTUAL SIZE

Colonies in tropical regions can contain millions of ants. Some, such as driver and army ants, eat almost anything and can strip a tethered horse to its skeleton.

FACT FILE

Scientific name
Formicidae family

Habitat Underground and compost heaps

Breeding Queens lay thousands of eggs every month

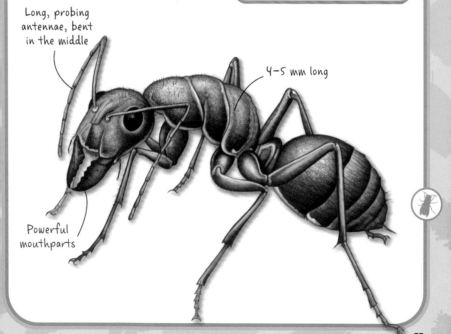

Long, probing antennae, bent in the middle

4–5 mm long

Powerful mouthparts

BEE

One of the most important groups of insect, bees benefit gardeners and farmers. They pollinate many plants, which is an essential part of fruit and seed production. Garden bumble bees, like honeybees, collect nectar from plants and feed pollen to their young. They are not aggressive insects and rarely sting. However unlike honeybees, bumblebees can sting more than once. Some types of bumblebee are in danger of becoming extinct.

ACTUAL SIZE

Bees communicate with each other in different ways, including 'dancing'. Honeybees returning to the hive use a dance to tell other bees where to find nectar.

FACT FILE

Scientific name *Apidae* family

Habitat Gardens, woodlands and parks

Breeding Queens lay more than 100 eggs a day

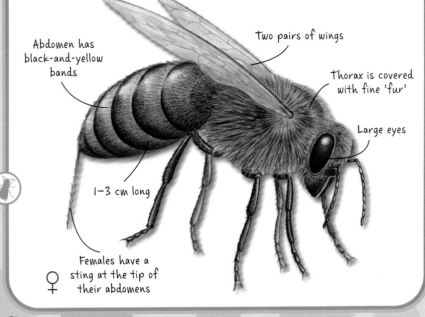

Abdomen has black-and-yellow bands

Two pairs of wings

Thorax is covered with fine 'fur'

Large eyes

1–3 cm long

♀ Females have a sting at the tip of their abdomens

GALL WASP

Gall wasps are not easy to find, but they leave very interesting clues behind after mating, which are simple to spot. These tiny insects lay eggs inside plants, often on oak trees, and by a process that remains a mystery, they make the plant tissues grow and swell. A gall is formed, which protects and feeds the growing larvae inside. Different types of gall wasp produce galls of different sizes and shapes. These insects are related to wasps, bees and ants.

ACTUAL SIZE

There are more than 1250 species of gall wasp, many of them in Europe and North America. Some gall wasps are tiny, growing no bigger than one mm.

FACT FILE

Scientific name
Cynips quercusfolii

Habitat Oak woodlands

Breeding Breed using galls, or swellings, on trees that protect the growing larvae

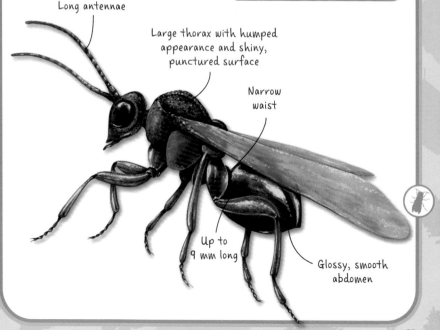

Long antennae

Large thorax with humped appearance and shiny, punctured surface

Narrow waist

Up to 9 mm long

Glossy, smooth abdomen

HORNTAIL

These fierce looking insects are sometimes called wood wasps and, although they look like stinging wasps, they are harmless. The long spike from a female's abdomen may appear to be a sting, but is actually an ovipositor – an organ the female uses to lay her eggs into wood. The larvae have small legs and strong mouthparts. They live inside a tree and feed on its wood for up to two years before turning into pupae.

ACTUAL SIZE

Female horntails are black and yellow. The males have an orange abdomen, with a black tip, and orange legs. They are smaller than the females.

FACT FILE

Scientific name
Urocerus gigas

Habitat Conifer woodlands

Breeding Eggs are laid in trunks

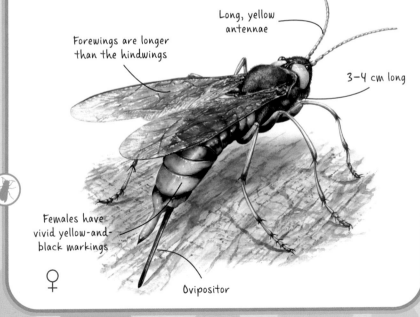

Long, yellow antennae

Forewings are longer than the hindwings

3–4 cm long

Females have vivid yellow-and-black markings

♀

Ovipositor

WASP

Common wasps live in large colonies, in a big nest made out of chewed wood fibres. They often choose to nest near or in houses and may become troublesome, because they can inflict painful stings. Queens are the only females that reproduce and they come out of hibernation in spring, ready to start a new colony. The first eggs she lays produce female workers, and later on her eggs produce males and new queens.

ACTUAL SIZE

Wasps belong to the same family of insects as bees and ants. Larvae feed on insects and adults feed on nectar or other sugary substances, such as rotting fruit.

FACT FILE

Scientific name
Vespula vulgaris

Habitat Gardens and woodlands

Breeding Larvae grow in cells or 'combs'

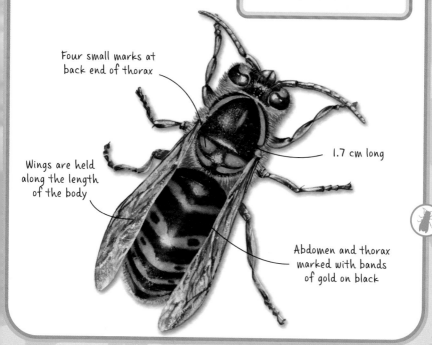

Four small marks at back end of thorax

Wings are held along the length of the body

1.7 cm long

Abdomen and thorax marked with bands of gold on black

BLUEBOTTLE

Easily recognized by the shiny metallic sheen to their bodies, bluebottles belong to a group of insects called blowflies. They visit gardens where there is rubbish, food or animal faeces, and they are unwelcome visitors since they spread diseases. When the eggs hatch, small, white carrot-shaped maggots emerge to feed and grow. The maggots dig into the ground and pupate, emerging as adult flies about ten days later.

ACTUAL SIZE

Blowflies eat the flesh of living animals. They lay their eggs in open wounds, the maggots hatch within eight hours, and then eat the flesh.

FACT FILE

Scientific name
Calliphora vomitoria
Habitat Gardens and houses
Breeding Larvae are called maggots

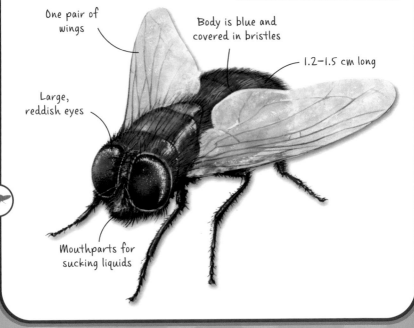

One pair of wings

Body is blue and covered in bristles

1.2–1.5 cm long

Large, reddish eyes

Mouthparts for sucking liquids

COMMON GNAT

Gnats are very common insects and they make a familiar humming sound when they fly at night. The adults lay their eggs in layers, called rafts, on the surface of water. When the larvae hatch they hang from the surface, then sink to the bottom of the body of water when they turn into pupae. The adults are able to survive cold winters by hibernating.

ACTUAL SIZE

FACT FILE

Scientific name
Culex pipiens
Habitat Open areas
Breeding Larvae live in water

Gnats sometimes bite humans, but they mostly bite birds, which in turn eat gnats.

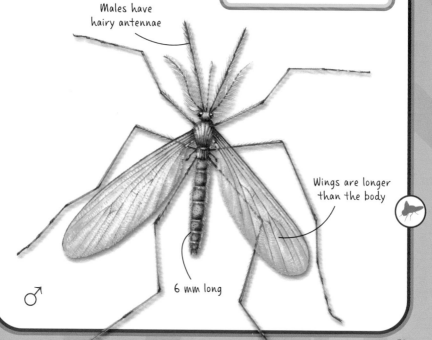

Males have hairy antennae

Wings are longer than the body

6 mm long

♂

39

CRANE FLY

Crane flies are more commonly known as daddy-long-legs. They have long, slender bodies and unusually long legs. In tropical regions, their legs can measure up to 10 cm, but 3–6 cm is normal in cooler places. Adults are usually seen in gardens in autumn, especially during periods of damp or foggy weather. The larvae live in soil, where they feed on roots.

ACTUAL SIZE

Crane flies are slow and easy to catch. They have small balancing limbs, called halteres, on either side of their bodies, which help to keep them stable when they fly.

FACT FILE

Scientific name
Tipula paludosa

Habitat Grasslands and gardens

Breeding Larvae are called leatherjackets, due to their tough, leathery skin

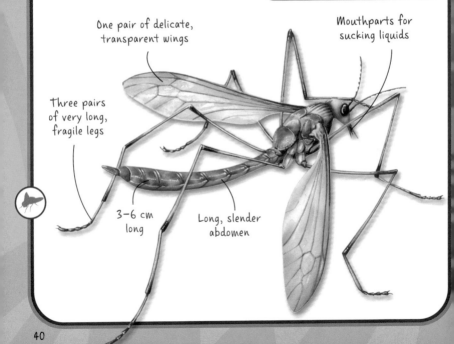

One pair of delicate, transparent wings

Mouthparts for sucking liquids

Three pairs of very long, fragile legs

3–6 cm long

Long, slender abdomen

FRUIT FLY

Fruit flies are one of the most common insects around homes, especially in the summer months. They lay their tiny eggs – up to 500 a time – on ripe or rotting fruit. The eggs can develop and hatch into larvae just one day after being laid, and they can grow into adults in just one week, if the weather is warm enough.

ACTUAL SIZE

These small insects are attracted to fruit, so they often live in kitchens or near fruit trees.

FACT FILE

Scientific name
Drosophila funebris

Habitat Composts and any rotting plants

Breeding Eggs are laid on rotting material

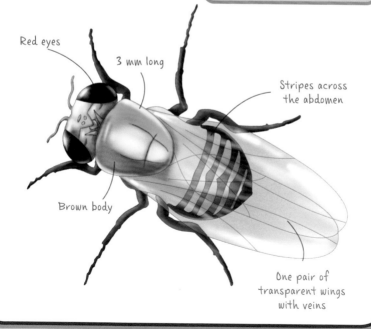

Red eyes

3 mm long

Stripes across the abdomen

Brown body

One pair of transparent wings with veins

HORSE FLY

There are more than 4000 species of horse fly in the world and they are amongst the largest of all flies. In Britain they are often found near wet habitats or around farms. The females bite humans or other animals and have razor-sharp mouthparts for cutting skin. They bite to get protein, which helps them produce bigger and healthier clusters of eggs. However the males suck nectar. The larvae are maggots, which live in mud and feed on rotting matter or small insects.

ACTUAL SIZE

Females use their enormous eyes to help them find their prey to bite. They can also detect carbon dioxide, the gas that humans and other animals breathe out.

FACT FILE

Scientific name
Tabanidae family

Habitat Woodland, rivers and marshes

Breeding Females lay up to 1000 eggs in a mass

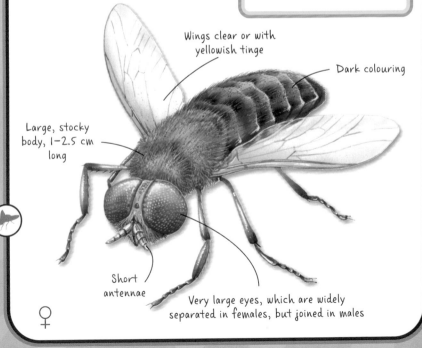

Wings clear or with yellowish tinge

Dark colouring

Large, stocky body, 1–2.5 cm long

Short antennae

Very large eyes, which are widely separated in females, but joined in males

♀

HOVERFLY

Skilled flyers, hoverflies only have one pair of wings, and they dart about and change direction with speed. Adults are often seen near flowering plants, making a high-pitched buzzing sound as they forage for nectar and pollen. They can hover in one place, with their wings beating so fast that the movement cannot be seen by the human eye.

ACTUAL SIZE

Hoverfly larvae emerge from small, white, oval eggs. They are blind and limbless, and have enormous appetites. Several generations hatch in one year.

FACT FILE

Scientific name
Syrphus ribesii

Habitat Gardens, parks and woodlands

Breeding Green or yellow sluglike larvae

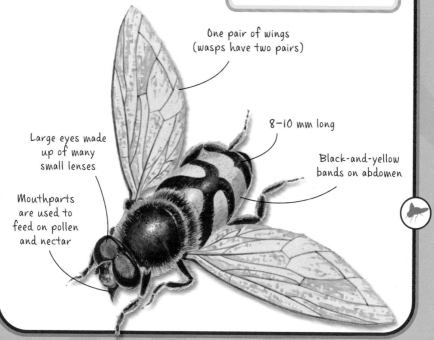

One pair of wings
(wasps have two pairs)

8–10 mm long

Black-and-yellow
bands on abdomen

Large eyes made
up of many
small lenses

Mouthparts
are used to
feed on pollen
and nectar

43

MOSQUITO

In spring, adults emerge from the water where they have lived as larvae. They can survive until winter and some adults hibernate. Males feed on nectar and other plant juices, but females need blood meals before they can lay their eggs. Mosquitoes have long mouthparts that they use to pierce skin (human or animal) and suck up blood. They are found near ponds, rivers and stagnant pools of water.

ACTUAL SIZE

In hot regions of the world, mosquitoes spread deadly diseases, such as malaria and dengue fever, to people. Only female Anopheles mosquitoes spread malaria.

FACT FILE

Scientific name
Aedes detritus

Habitat Near slow-moving or still water

Breeding Larvae live in water

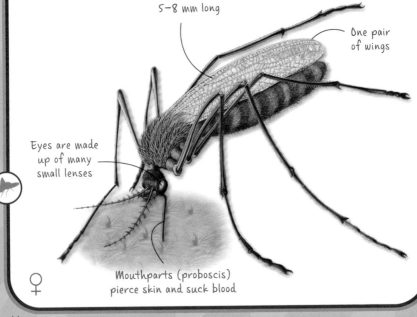

5–8 mm long

One pair of wings

Eyes are made up of many small lenses

♀

Mouthparts (proboscis) pierce skin and suck blood

COMMON BLUE DAMSELFLY

Damselflies rest with their wings folded along the length of their bodies, unlike dragonflies, which spread their wings out. Male and female common blue damselflies look different, as the females have bluish or yellowish bodies. These insects sometimes fly in large groups over ponds and slow-flowing rivers, hunting for other insects to eat.

ACTUAL SIZE

Nymphs live in water and crawl out on plant stems when they are ready to fly as adults.

FACT FILE

Scientific name
Enallogama cyathigerum

Habitat Near water

Breeding Larvae are called nymphs

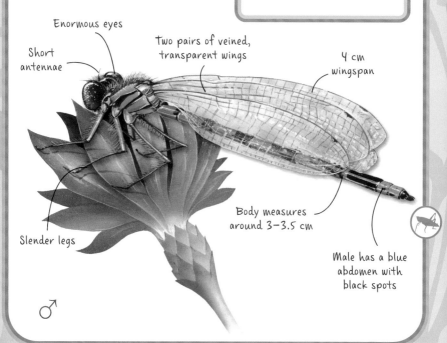

Enormous eyes

Short antennae

Two pairs of veined, transparent wings

4 cm wingspan

Slender legs

Body measures around 3–3.5 cm

Male has a blue abdomen with black spots

♂

COMMON COCKROACH

Cockroaches are very common insects, but it is unusual to see one. They are nocturnal, which means they are most active at night, and they move fast if they sense anyone is around. After mating, the females (which cannot fly) leave their eggs in a warm, dry place to mature. The newly hatched cockroaches are called nymphs and they do not have wings.

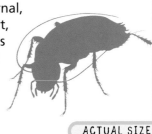

ACTUAL SIZE

These creatures feed on rubbish and rotting material, and are known to spread disease.

FACT FILE

Scientific name
Blatta orientalis

Habitat Houses and warm places

Breeding 16 eggs are laid in an egg case

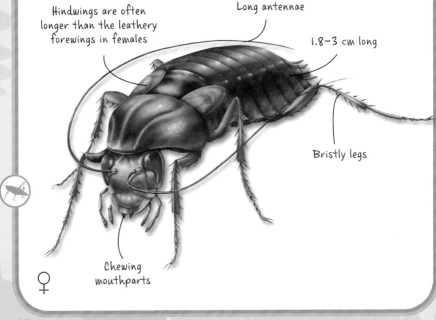

Hindwings are often longer than the leathery forewings in females

Long antennae

1.8–3 cm long

Bristly legs

Chewing mouthparts

♀

DRAGONFLY

Dragonflies are superb flyers and dart around in summer and autumn, visiting woodlands and gardens where there is water. They can be easily recognized by their long, slender bodies with colourful bands. Dragonflies have huge eyes that almost meet, and give them great vision. These insects spend most of their early lives underwater in ponds or lakes as nymphs. They breathe using gills.

ACTUAL SIZE

In ancient times, dragonflies were much bigger than they are today. Fossils of dragonflies show that their wingspans reached up to 75 cm!

FACT FILE

Scientific name
Odonata order

Habitat Near slow-moving or still water

Breeding Nymphs feed on fish, tadpoles and other small aquatic animals

Two pairs of long, slender wings

Huge eyes that cover most of the head

Males have claspers at the tips of their abdomens

2–9 cm long

Coloured body with ten segments

♂

EARWIG

Plentiful in most gardens, earwigs are often found lurking in cracks and crevices where it is dark and they are hidden from predators. They have long, thin bodies and two pairs of wings – the first of which are leathery and short. Earwigs have pincers, called cerci, on the ends of their abdomen. Cerci are used to help fold the wings back after flight.

ACTUAL SIZE

It was once believed that earwigs climbed into people's ears and burrowed into the brain. Mashed earwigs were used in Roman times to treat earache.

FACT FILE

Scientific name
Forficula auricularia

Habitat In soil and under stones

Breeding Young earwigs appear white when they moult

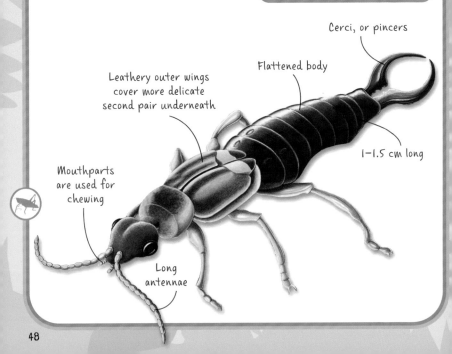

Cerci, or pincers

Flattened body

Leathery outer wings cover more delicate second pair underneath

1–1.5 cm long

Mouthparts are used for chewing

Long antennae

GRASSHOPPER

With their large wings, grasshoppers are **good flyers, but they prefer to escape from danger by leaping.** Usually green, they are well camouflaged against foliage. They have long, powerful legs that they use for jumping more than 20 times their own body length. Crickets have longer antennae than grasshoppers and can often be heard 'singing' on a summer's evening. The song sounds like a series of loud 'chirrups'.

ACTUAL SIZE

In some parts of the world grasshoppers are a popular food. Their legs and wings are removed before the body is fried in oil.

FACT FILE

Scientific name
Orthoptera order

Habitat Grasslands, gardens and woodlands

Breeding Larvae are called nymphs

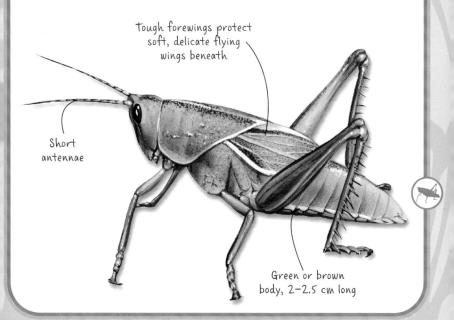

Tough forewings protect soft, delicate flying wings beneath

Short antennae

Green or brown body, 2–2.5 cm long

LACEWING

Green lacewings have slender, delicate bodies and long, flimsy wings that are veined and almost transparent. There are more than 1600 species of lacewing and most of them are only active at night. They are predators and attack all sorts of other insects, especially those with soft bodies, such as caterpillars and aphids. For this reason, they are often bred in large numbers and released on farmland to reduce the number of pests, without the need for chemical pesticides.

ACTUAL SIZE

Lacewings are equipped with sensors on their wings. These can detect ultrasound, which is a type of noise produced by bats, so lacewings can avoid being eaten by them.

FACT FILE

Scientific name
Chrysopidae family

Habitat Woodland, farms and gardens

Breeding Eggs are laid on long stalks to protect them from ants and other predators

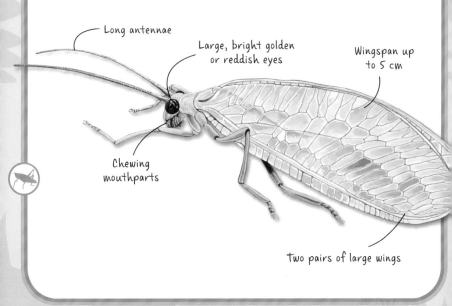

Long antennae

Large, bright golden or reddish eyes

Wingspan up to 5 cm

Chewing mouthparts

Two pairs of large wings

SCORPION FLY

Scorpion flies mostly feed on dead insects and they have tough, biting mouthparts that can tackle crunchy skins. They find their food in spiders' webs. The males have swollen tails that look like scorpion stingers. In fact, these organs are used during mating. Female scorpion flies sometimes like to eat their mates, so males present them with a gift of a drop of saliva before mating, to prevent an untimely death.

ACTUAL SIZE

Both adults and larvae eat dead animals, especially insects and plants.

FACT FILE

Scientific name
Panorpa communis

Habitat: Gardens, woodlands and hedgerows

Breeding: Larvae resemble caterpillars

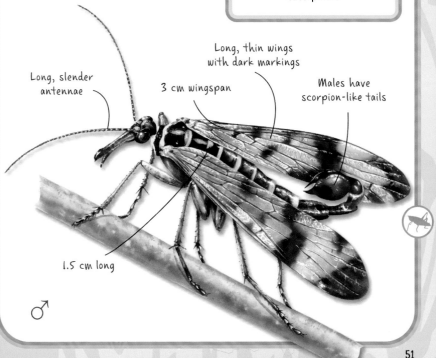

Long, slender antennae

Long, thin wings with dark markings

3 cm wingspan

Males have scorpion-like tails

1.5 cm long

♂

SILVERFISH

Silverfish are very common insects and it is easiest to see them at night, when they are most active. They prefer damp habitats, such as bathrooms. Silverfish scavenge whatever food they can find, but mostly eat starchy food, such as mould, paper, flour and glue. The nymphs that hatch from eggs moult many times before becoming adults.

ACTUAL SIZE

These tough little insects have been known to survive for a whole year without food.

FACT FILE

Scientific name
Lepisma saccharina
Habitat Houses and sheds
Breeding Small nymphs

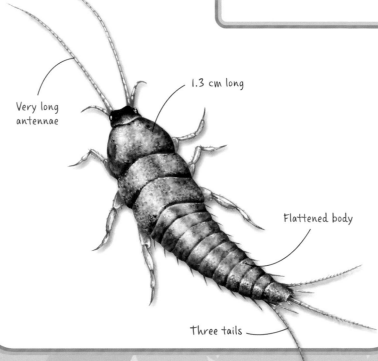

Very long antennae

1.3 cm long

Flattened body

Three tails

SPECKLED BUSH CRICKET

These insects are the smallest British crickets, but they are common. The adults feed on leaves through the summer, especially on those from rose and raspberry bushes. Other crickets stop chirping in late summer, but speckled bush crickets make their soft noises well into autumn, although they can be hard to hear.

ACTUAL SIZE

Most crickets have two pairs of working wings, but a speckled bush cricket's wings are too small to be of any use.

FACT FILE

Scientific name
Leptophyes punctatissima

Habitat Grasslands, gardens and parks

Breeding Eggs are laid in cracks in bark

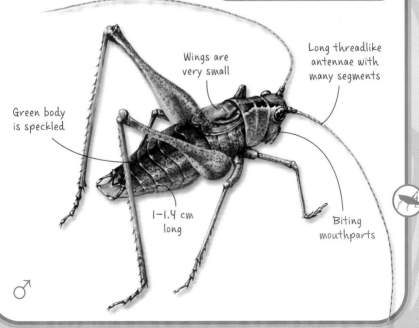

Wings are very small

Long threadlike antennae with many segments

Green body is speckled

1–1.4 cm long

Biting mouthparts

♂

TWO-TAILED BRISTLETAIL

These insects are easy to confuse with earwigs, as they have two thread-like growths at their tail ends and long, slender bodies. Two-tailed bristletails eat other insects or rotting plant matter that they come across. Females lay many eggs in a hole in the ground and, when they hatch, the little larvae look just like their parents.

ACTUAL SIZE

FACT FILE

Scientific name
Campodea fragilis

Habitat Compost heaps and rotting vegetation

Breeding Young are nymphs

Bristletails do not have eyes and must rely on their other senses to find food.

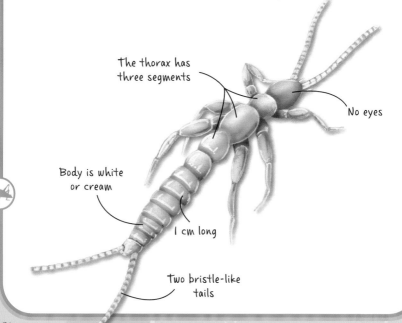

The thorax has three segments

No eyes

Body is white or cream

1 cm long

Two bristle-like tails

WHITEFLY

There are many different types of whitefly that attack garden plants, house plants and greenhouse plants. They lay their eggs on the leaves of their host and both the larvae and adults feed on sap, causing some damage but also passing viruses between plants. Tens of thousands of whitefly can live on a single tree or vegetable crop. Whiteflies have a very short life cycle and can go from egg to adult in just three weeks.

ACTUAL SIZE

Whiteflies are attracted to yellow, so gardeners sometimes plant marigolds near their crops to encourage the whitefly to feed on them instead.

FACT FILE

Scientific name
Aleyrodes species
Habitat Farms and gardens
Breeding Larvae are called nymphs

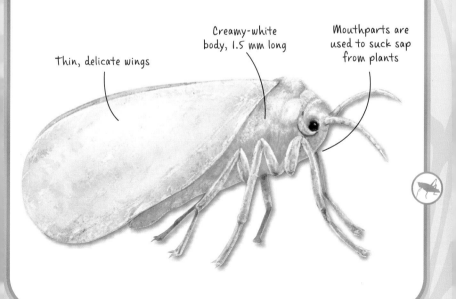

Thin, delicate wings

Creamy-white body, 1.5 mm long

Mouthparts are used to suck sap from plants

GLOSSARY

Abdomen The rear part of an insect's body, behind the head and thorax.

Antennae (singular: antenna) A pair of structures on an insect's head, sensitive to smell, sound and touch.

Camouflage The way that an animal's colour, markings or shape enables it to blend in with its surroundings.

Caterpillar A moth or butterfly larva.

Cerci Sensory projections at the end of the abdomen of some insects.

Chrysalis (plural: chrysalises) A hard case that protects the pupa of an insect, especially a butterfly or moth.

Colony A group of insects that live together and are all offspring of the same female – the queen.

Compound eyes Eyes that are made up of many small lenses.

Elytra The wing cases of a beetle.

Exoskeleton The tough, waterproof casing of an insect's body.

Habitat The natural home of a plant or animal.

Hibernate To spend the winter in a deep sleep.

Larvae (singular: larva) The first stage of an insect's life-cycle after hatching from its egg.

Maggot The larva of a fly.

Mandibles An insect's main pair of jaws, which chop up food.

Migrate To travel in search of food, better weather or breeding sites.

Moulting Shedding an old skin, to reveal a new skin underneath.

Nectar A sugary liquid produced by plants that attracts pollinating insects, such as bees and wasps.

Nymph The larvae of insects such as dragonflies and grasshoppers.

Overwinter To spend winter in a way that allows insects to remain alive through the cold period. Hibernation and migration are the two main ways to overwinter.

Ovipositor A female insect's egg-laying organ.

Proboscis The tube-like mouthparts of moths, butterflies and some flies.

Pupa (plural: pupae) The resting stage of an insect's life-cycle, when it changes from a larva to an adult.

Queen An egg-laying female in a colony of ants, bees or wasps.

Sap A nutrient-rich liquid found in plants.

Species A group of similar living things that can breed together.

Thorax The middle section of an insect's body, where the legs and wings (if there are any) are attached.

Workers The insects in a colony that build the nest, find food and care for the young. Workers cannot breed. There are worker bees and ants.